Owl nests are often found in trees, barns, rocky or grassy places.

3

WARM AND SAFE

OWLS AND OWLETS

By Annabelle Lynch

Contents

W

FRANKLIN WATTS

LONDON·SYDNEY

LAYING AN EGG

Baby owls are called owlets. They hatch from **eggs**.

When a mother owl is ready to lay eggs, she builds a **nest**.

2

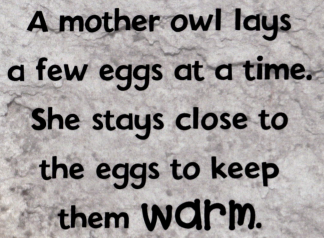

A mother owl lays a few eggs at a time. She stays close to the eggs to keep them **warm**.

After about thirty days, the eggs are ready to **hatch**.

HATCHING

Each owlet hatches at a different time. They use a special sharp point on their beak, called an **egg tooth**, to help break the egg shell.

Newborn owlets are blind and helpless.

Their mother and father stay close to keep them safe.

BIG EYES

Owlets open their eyes about ten days after they hatch.

They have very **big** eyes that help them to see well.

8

Owls can't move their **eyes** easily.

Instead, they can turn their **head** to see all around them.

9

FUZZ AND FEATHERS

Owlets don't have any feathers when they hatch. Instead, they have a **fuzzy** covering called down.

In a few weeks, owlets
start growing feathers.

Flap!

Flap!

Different owls have different
coloured feathers. They help the owl
to blend in with its surroundings.

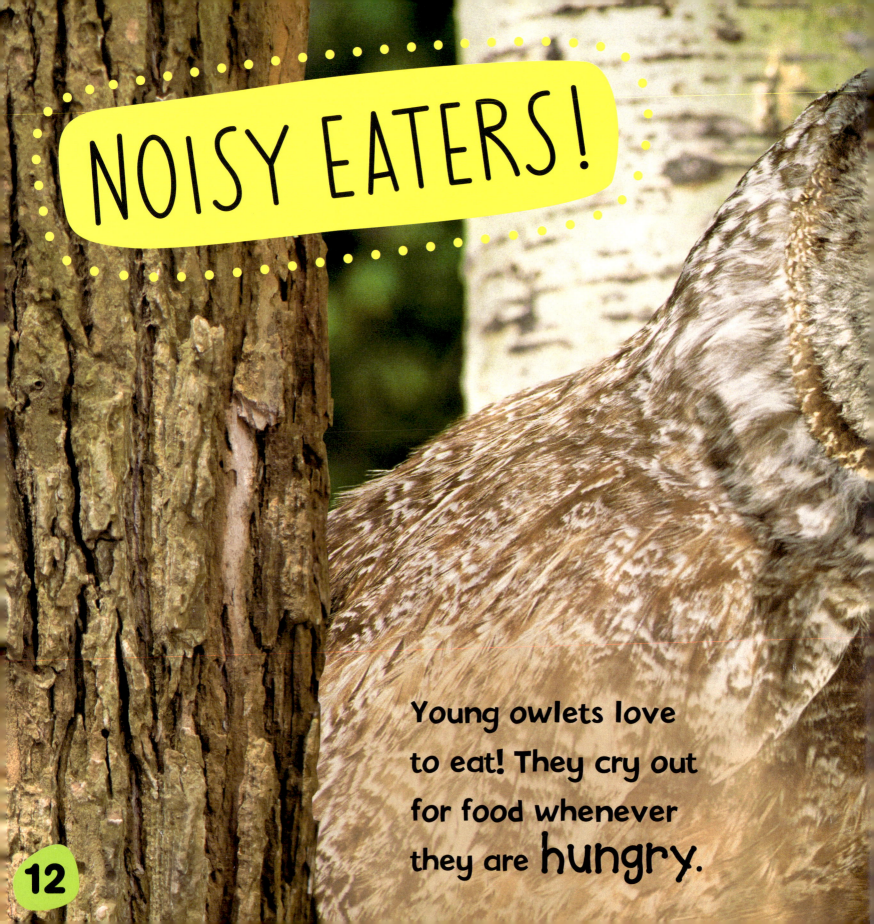

NOISY EATERS!

Young owlets love to eat! They cry out for food whenever they are **hungry**.

Their parents bring them food many times a day. Owlets eat small **animals**, such as mice, rabbits, birds, frogs and insects.

Yum! Yum!

13

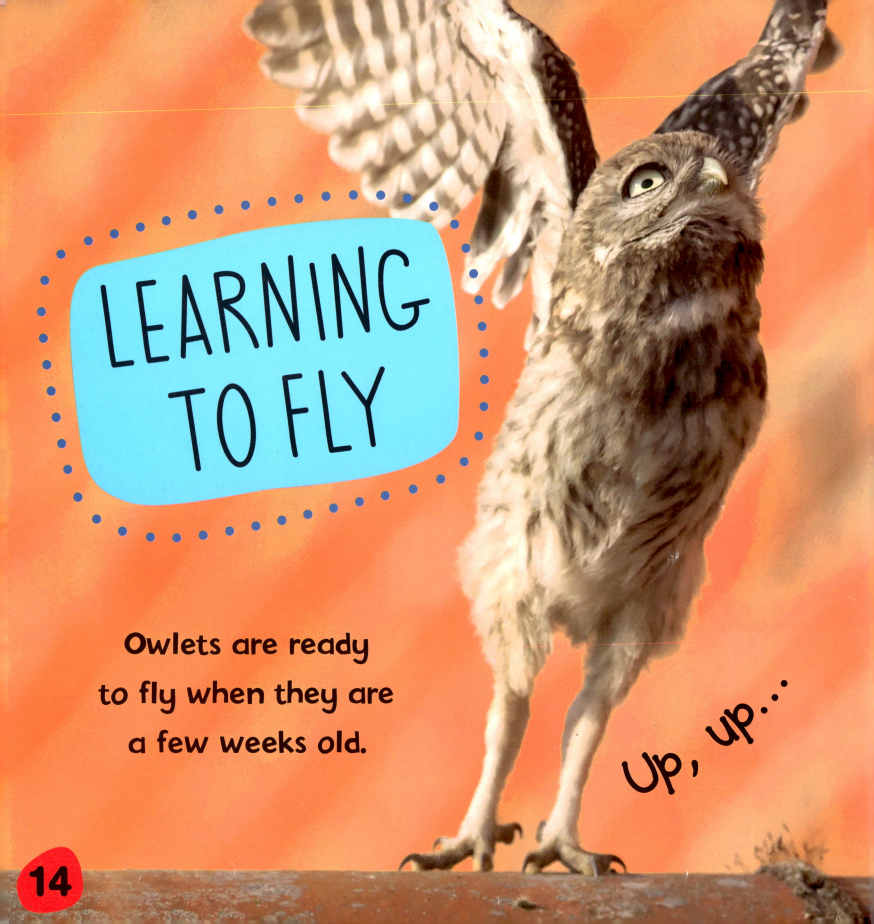

LEARNING TO FLY

Owlets are ready
to fly when they are
a few weeks old.

up, up...

Owlets learn how to fly by watching their parents. At first, they can't fly too far because they get a bit tired!

...and away!

15

BEAK AND CLAWS

As owlets grow up, they learn how to **catch** food for themselves.

16

Their **sharp** claws, called talons, help them to snatch up their food.

Their **hooked** beak helps them to tear their food into little pieces.

pellet

Owls swallow their food whole. The bits that they can't eat, such as bones or fur, are made into **pellets**. The owl spits these out.

NIGHT OWLS

Most owls **rest** during the day and hunt for food at night.

Zzzz

Their big eyes help them to see in the dark. Owls fly very quietly. This helps them to sneak up on little animals and pounce!

FLYING THE NEST

As they grow up, owls can
fly further and further.
They are soon ready to leave their parents.

20

Most owls settle far away from their home nest, where there is more chance of finding food.

At around a year old, owls are ready to have owlets of their own.

AN OWL'S LIFE CYCLE

hatching out

a few weeks old

four months old

a grown-up owl

22

down

egg tooth

hatch

feathers

WORD BANK

nest

pellet

23

INDEX

24

Franklin Watts
Published in paperback in Great Britain in 2019
by The Watts Publishing Group

Series Editor: Julia Bird
Series Designer: Basement 68

Picture credits: Anuwat/Shutterstock: 12l. Maisan Caines/ Dreamstime: 10, 23tl. Jules Cox/FLPA: 1bl, 9.Sergey Gorshkov/ FLPA: 11. HERGON/Shutterstock: 19. Issele/Dreamstime: 22br. Eric Isselee/Shutterstock: 8, 23tc. Wayne Lynch/All Canada Photos/Alamy: back cover tr, 12–13, 24. Derek Middleton/FLPA: front cover. Jerome Murray-CC/Alamy: 14, 22tr. picturepartners/ Shutterstock: 17, 23b. Michael Quinton/Minden Pictures/FLPA: 6, 22tl, 23tr. Paul Reeves Photography/Shutterstock: 18, 23cl. Andy Rouse/Nature PL: 20–21, 22bl. Tui de Roy/Minden Pictures/FLPA: back cover tl, 7, 23cr. Tui de Roy/Nature PL: 7. Vasily Vashnevskiy/Shutterstock: 1tr, 2–3, 5r. John Waters/Nature PL: 16. Martin B Withers/FLPA: 15.

Every attempt has been made to clear copyright. Should there be any inadvertent omission please apply to the publisher for rectification.

ISBN 978 1 4451 4885 4

Printed in China

MIX
Paper from responsible sources
FSC® C104740

Franklin Watts
An imprint of
Hachette Children's Group
Part of The Watts Publishing Group
Carmelite House
50 Victoria Embankment
London EC4Y 0DZ

An Hachette UK Company
www.hachette.co.uk

www.franklinwatts.co.uk